Divine Reminders

Scott Curran

Divine Reminders
copyright 2014 by Scott Curran

To you, my friend in God.

Contents

Introduction

Divine Reminders is a collection of three of my previously-published ebooks:

Living in Spiritual Consciousness

Awareness of God's Presence

Total Gratitude

Each of the three books is written from the point of view of God speaking to you.

The books are available individually as ebooks or in this three-book collection called Divine Reminders, which is available both in ebook format and in paperback.

Peace be with you, my spiritual friend.

Living in Spiritual Consciousness

To you -- my friend in Spirit.

Contents

Introduction

Living in Spiritual Consciousness is about losing our false life and finding our true life in God. It's about surrendering our life to God and seeing God's loving will in all that occurs. It's written from the point of view of God speaking to you.

Chapter 1 - Accepting Everything

Living in spiritual consciousness means accepting everything.

See my loving will in all that occurs.

Accept everything with equanimity.

Accept, with equanimity, the fact that you don't always accept everything with equanimity.

Accept that you sometimes act foolishly.

Accept that you sometimes worry.

Accept that you sometimes don't know what to do.

Accept that you sometimes get frustrated and angry.

You're human. You mess up sometimes.

Accept yourself as you are.

Accept others as they are.

Accept all that is -- as it is.

No criticisms and no complaints.

Trusting in me, just give thanks.

Let trials and annoyances bring you beyond your self.

If you're criticized, ridiculed or judged harshly, it doesn't matter.

Lose your life in the realization that your true life is in me.

Things such as illnesses, setbacks, delays, discordant people and upheavals are tickets to paradise.

Every trial is an opportunity for you to take up your cross, die to self and enter into the awareness of your eternal life in me.

You can get angry or you can trust me and be peaceful.

Whatever occurs is my perfect will.

Every single thing that has ever happened in your life is my will.

Everything is bringing you to union with me.

Welcome everything and everyone.

When faced with annoyances, sufferings, discomforts, difficulties, trials and catastrophes, say, "Thank you, Lord. I don't understand why this is happening, but I trust that whatever happens is your will and that you will only what's best."

Totally abandon yourself to my will.

Accept everything as it is and be at peace.

Chapter 2 - Avoiding Judging

Living in spiritual consciousness means avoiding judging.

Give thanks for what is -- just as it is.

Why get embroiled?

Why meddle in the lives of other people?

Have an attitude of non-attachment.

Mind your own business.

I'm in control of everything and I know what I'm doing.

Whether it's raining or sunny, hot or cold, why judge the climate as being good or bad? It is what it is. That's all it is.

Whether you're tired or well-rested, whether you're ill or in good health, you are what you are.

Accept what is.

Why complain or make judgements about what is?

Give thanks in all conditions and circumstances. Yes, even those conditions and circumstances that, from a worldly perspective, seem terrible.

Everything is for the best.

If you realize that you were judging, don't condemn yourself for judging.

If you were judging, just acknowledge it and let it go.

Don't judge another person's motives.

Do you know why a person does what they do?

Do you even know why you yourself do what you do?

Don't judge others and don't judge yourself.

Don't be concerned about how others judge you. It doesn't matter.

Live and let live.

In spiritual consciousness, you avoid judging.

Chapter 3 - Dying to Illusion

Living in spiritual consciousness means dying to illusion.

Things aren't what they seem.

The world of your ego is a world of illusion.

Why compare yourself with others?

You are what you are.

They are what they are.

In spiritual consciousness, you realize who you are in me.

You have my mind.   I'm the Consciousness of your Consciousness.

Trade the world of illusion for the realm of reality -- the kingdom of God, the kingdom of heaven. See my loving will in all that occurs and in all that doesn't occur.

Dying to self, you die to illusion.

My thoughts and ways aren't like yours.

Your thoughts and perceptions are only thoughts and perceptions. They aren't reality.

Realize -- this isn't real.

When faced with conditions that could rankle you, let your attitude be -- If I wasn't dead, that might bother me.

As you become nothing -- illusions vanish.

You're being transformed, like a caterpillar that becomes a butterfly!

Chapter 4 - Living in the Truth

Living in spiritual consciousness means living in the truth.

Knowing the truth sets you free.

I'm truth.

I'm love.

Know me. In the awareness of your oneness with me, you live in truth and love.

You're spirit.

You're eternal.

Apart from me, you're nothing, and you can do nothing.

I love you -- yes, I know your worldly weaknesses, wickedness and weirdness.

In me, you're not of the world anymore than I'm of the world.

I'm manifesting as you, and as everyone else too.

I'm the only reality.

If it isn't me, then it isn't real. It's illusion.

I'm the Unseen Essence of all that is.

You're in the midst of an amazing mystery.

All is one in me.

In me, you're one with all.

In spiritual consciousness, you relax and rejoice in the truth.

Chapter 5 - Living with Humility

Living in spiritual consciousness means living with humility.

Be happy to say, "I don't know."

Be happy when others are praised.

Be happy to live and die in obscurity.

Be happy when you're excluded.

Be happy when you're insulted.

Be happy when your ego is taking a beating.

You're becoming humble.

You're becoming nothing.

You're becoming real.

Be happy when you're ridiculed, maligned, and persecuted.

Be happy to be last.

Be happy to serve.

In humility, you give glory to me.

Only in me do you find peace.

The peace that you have in me isn't based on the opinions of other people or on external events.

In the awareness of your nothingness, you have humility.

I'm all.

I'm love.

In spiritual consciousness, you're gentle and humble.

You live with humility.

Chapter 6 - Knowing That You're Forgiven and Being Forgiving

Living in spiritual consciousness means knowing that you're forgiven and being forgiving.

Forgive as I have forgiven you.

Forgive everyone.

Forgive yourself.

Forgive yourself for the times you've been unforgiving.

Trust in my mercy and love.

Be forgiving and loving.

What's impossible for you is possible with me.

In me, you can forgive.

In me, you can love.

Why play the blame game?

Don't look back.

What happened is what happened.

What's happening is what's happening.

Everything that occurs in your life is my will for you, and I will only what is best for you.

Right now is all there is.

It's always now.

You're forgiven.

Forgive.

Chapter 7 - Being Dead to Self

Living in spiritual consciousness means being dead to self.

Things such as delays, disappointments, annoyances and disasters are part of your earthly life. Accept them as my holy and perfect will for you.

Being dead to self, you're alive to a new life in me -- here and now.

Accept whatever happened in the past without ruminating about it.

It was what it was.

You're dead, so it doesn't matter.

Why beat yourself up when you're already dead?

Why get frustrated with yourself for not yet being dead enough?

Your sanctification is my work.

Apart from me, you can do nothing.

Accept that you sometimes forget reality and slip into illusion.

You're a citizen of heaven.

You're not of the world of illusion any more than I am of the world of illusion.

In knowing me -- in being spiritually conscious -- you've crossed over from death to life.

Knowing me is eternal life.

You're in the kingdom of heaven.

28

The 'flesh' -- your worldly self and your mortal mind -- counts for nothing.

You are infinite spirit.

Chapter 8 - Being Dead to the World

Living in spiritual consciousness means being dead to the world.

Why would you need approval or status?

Being dead to your self you're dead to the world.

Do you need a lot of stuff? What for?

Do you need guilt, shame, resentment and blame?

Why not get rid of what you don't need?

Look at whatever it is from a cosmic perspective.

Why get embroiled in the stories and scenes of your mortal mind?

In spiritual consciousness, you're dead to the world and alive in my kingdom.

Chapter 9 - Being in the Kingdom of Heaven

Living in spiritual consciousness means being in the kingdom of heaven.

You're in my kingdom -- 'the kingdom of heaven,' 'the kingdom of God.'

Thoughts are just thoughts. That's all they are.

Thoughts aren't real. They're just thoughts.

Spiritual consciousness -- my kingdom -- is beyond thoughts.

My kingdom is within you.

Be -- unselfconscious.

The price of admission into my kingdom is -- your life.

Surrender your will and your life to me.

By losing your life, you find your real life in me.

Why not trade your illusions -- your thoughts, your stories, your judgements, your fears, your desires, your biases, your conditioning, your preferences -- for Truth?

Instead of relying on your mortal mind, put your trust in me.

You sometimes wonder why this or that is the way it is, or why he or she is the way they are, or why this or that happened or didn't happen. Just trust in me and forget about why.

Be at peace with what is, as it is.

Love people as they are.

Things that seem to be killing you are bringing you to eternal life in me.

Eternal life is this -- to know me, to be conscious of me.

Trade your thoughts and ways for mine.

In spiritual consciousness, your will is aligned with mine.

My will is done on earth as it is in heaven.

Be content with whatever happens or doesn't happen.

Be content with whatever is or isn't.

Make a decision to abandon yourself to me.

In spiritual consciousness, you're in my kingdom.

Chapter 10 - Trusting in the Spirit

Living in spiritual consciousness means trusting in me.

I created you.

I don't need your directives or your advice.

Do you realize that, when you complain, you're saying that you know better than I do how things ought to be? How silly is that?

Why should everything be the way you think it should be?

Why should everyone think you're wonderful?

What does it matter what anyone thinks of you, one way or the other?

In the awareness of me, creatures are nothing.

Step back. Get out of the way.

I'll handle it. Okay?

Your ticket to peace is -- trusting me.

If you truly trusted in me, what would there be to worry about?

There's nothing to worry about. Nothing at all.

Why let your heart be troubled about anything?

Everything's fine.

Everything's perfect.

Cast your cares on me.

I'm the essence of every person, place and thing.

I'm operating in every circumstance.

Look with the vision of I within you -- and truly see.

Trust in me and watch things unfold -- perfectly.

Chapter 11 - Appreciating Mystery

Living in spiritual consciousness means appreciating mystery.

Know that you just don't know.

Accept that you don't know why things are the way they are.

Accept that you don't know why things happen the way they happen.

You don't need to know why.

Forget about why.

Say "I don't know" often, because it's true. You don't know.

You don't know anything.

What you do know is beyond thoughts and words.

Truth is -- experienced.

Ask yourself -- Who are you?

What are you?

Where are you?

What are you doing here?

Where is here? In relation to what?

How are you able to exist?

Why does your body die?

What happens to you after your body dies?

You don't know.

Life is a sublime mystery.

You don't have to figure it all out.

In spiritual consciousness, you delight in mystery.

Chapter 12 - Living with Non-Attachment

Living in spiritual consciousness means living with non-attachment.

You don't need anyone's approval.

If someone was unkind or unfair toward you, why make judgements about it?

All that happens is for a higher purpose and for your good.

Forgive and move on.

Often things happen for a reason that is beyond the ability of human reason to comprehend.

Things that seem to assault your sense of self are bringing you to a deeper awareness of your oneness with me.

In the world, you'll have troubles, but in me you have overcome the world.

You're in the world, but you're not of the world.

'The world,' -- 'the flesh,' -- counts for nothing.   It's transitory and illusory.

My timeless, infinite spirit is your life.

If you're praised and honored -- Amen.

If you're reviled and shunned -- Amen.

You're nothing apart from me.

In me, you're everything.

Leave outcomes to me.

Trusting in me, let your attitude be -- 'I'm at peace with whatever happens or doesn't happen.'

In spiritual consciousness, you trust in me, and you have an attitude of blessed non-attachment toward all people, things and events.

Chapter 13 - Appreciating Silence

Living in spiritual consciousness means appreciating silence.

Silence -- teaches.

Learn from silence.

To the interior tumult and chatter, say -- Peace. Be quiet.

Keep your words simple and few.

Listen more and speak less.

Go to quiet places.

Have a sanctuary of silence within.

Words can create barriers as well as bridges.

Often a smile, a nod, or a look communicates more effectively than spoken words.

Speaking can muffle the message of silence.

Talk less. Be silent more.

Communicate -- in silence.

Silence is your friend.

Though being in silence can be awkward at first, you soon get used to it.

Get to know silence. It's a beautiful companion.

Silence has much to say. Listen.

In spiritual consciousness, you appreciate silence.

Chapter 14 - Going with the Flow

Living in spiritual consciousness means going with the flow.

Why argue with what is? It is what it is.

What you resist you give more credence to.

Let difficult people and troubling situations dissolve in a sea of holy indifference.

Let the dramas of illusion dissipate into nothingness.

Let your attitude be -- Whatever happens, happens, and whatever is, is.

See my loving will in all that is and in all that happens -- in every detail of your life.

Take it easy.

Go slow.

Be like the river -- go with the flow.

Life is unfolding exactly as it's meant to unfold.

You're where you're supposed to be.

Turn your will and your life over to me.

Be at peace with everything as it is.

Accept and love yourself as you are, with your strengths and your weaknesses.

Accept and love others as they are.

Accept and love life as it is.

Give thanks in all situations.

I love you.

I'm in control of everything.

Leave everything to me.

Amen.

Awareness of God's Presence

To you, my friend in Spirit.

Contents

Introduction

Awareness of God's Presence is about forgetting our self and living out of the awareness of our oneness with God. It's about seeing God in everyone and everything. It's written from the point of view of God speaking to you.

Chapter 1 - Freedom

In the awareness of my presence, you're free.

Live in freedom.

Be your real self.

You don't have to impress anyone.

It doesn't matter if others approve or disapprove of you.

Enjoy silence.

In me, you're free of judging.

Go beyond fear and desire.

Go beyond self.

You're not of the world.

Be dead to the world.

Love, without self interest.

You're beyond space and time.

You're one with the Divine.

Banish regrets.

Accept my forgiveness.

Accept my love.

Forgive yourself and others.

Live by grace.

You're one with me.

I'm everywhere.

I'm everything.

I'm everyone.

I'm beyond all, through all and in all.

Where I am, there's freedom.

Everything's the way it's meant to be.

In the awareness of my presence, you have humility.

In humility, you're free.

Chapter 2 - Joy

In the awareness of my presence, you have joy.

Live in joy.

In me, there's infinite joy.

Being joyful doesn't mean that you're ecstatic all the time. It means that you trust me.

You're joyful in the midst of sorrow.

You're joyful in the midst of confusion.

In me, you're everywhere.

Being everywhere, you're joyful.

Joy dances in your heart.

Joy shines in the stars.

Joy laughs in a child.

Joy sparkles in the sunlight on the water.

Joy smiles in the sky.

The angels and saints in heaven are saying, "Hi!"

Though some things disturb and annoy, you still have joy.

Celebrate life.

Rejoice with celestial friends.

You're one with the Infinite Mind.

You're beyond space and time.

In me, you're joyful.

Chapter 3 - Peace

In the awareness of my presence, you have peace.

You don't have to control anything.

You can't control anything.

Leave everything to me.

Let go.

Get out of the way.

Look at everything in a new way.

See through my eyes.

In me, you're a new being.

You're light.

You're truth.

Let go of the notions of your ego.

You no longer live.

I'm living -- in you.

The veil of illusion is gone.

I'm your life.

You're nothing.

Don't worry about outcomes.

I'm in control.

There's no need to meddle.

61

There's no need to worry.

Live and let live.

Trust me.

Surrender your life to me.

Relax in the awareness of my presence.

You're already in eternity.

Take it easy.

Go slow.

You have your being in me.

Live in reality -- live in love.

Love is the only reality.

In me, you have peace.

My peace I give you.

Chapter 4 - Love

In the awareness of my presence, you know that I love you, and you love me and others.

I'm love.

In me, you love as I love.

My love flows through you.

Your worldly self is consumed in the fire of love.

Love rules the universe.

Love pervades the universe.

Love lifts you out of the pit whenever you slip into it.

Live in love.

Be kind and compassionate.

Be kind to yourself too.

Love yourself with all your weaknesses and flaws.

Love others the way they are.

You're not here to reform people. You're here to love them.

Love yourself and others as I love -- unconditionally.

Know my love.

I love you as you are -- yes, with all your human shortcomings.

My love for you is beyond anything you can imagine.

My spirit is working in you according to my good purpose.

Live in the awareness of my grace.

You're loved by me and, because of me, you're able to love.

In me, you love.

Chapter 5 - Gratitude

In the awareness of my presence, you have gratitude.

You appreciate everything.

Gratitude gives you perspective.

Gratitude makes the ordinary extraordinary.

Gratitude turns the mundane into something delightful.

Being thankful for everything, you're joyful always.

A heart that's grateful is a heart that's glad.

You're nothing. I'm everything.

Being aware of my presence and being empty of self, you're filled with wonder and joy.

Live in gratitude.

Continually consider your many blessings.

Be content with everything -- just the way it is.

Delight in my will.

Give thanks in all circumstances.

Chapter 6 - Eternal Life

In the awareness of my presence, you know that you have eternal life in me -- now.

Lose your life and have your life in me.

You're earthly life is short.

The troubles you experience in this world are temporary.

One day, there'll be no more sufferings or sorrows.

One day, by my grace, you'll be fully and forever in the Kingdom of Light.

What's visible is transitory.

What's invisible is eternal.

See through illusion.

See the Real.

Your physical form is changing and temporary. Your real self is timeless spirit.

Eternity is now.

Look at things from the perspective of eternity.

In the cosmic scheme of things, is this whatever it is really a big deal?

Your earthly life passes in the blink of an eye.

Don't get upset about the fact that you sometimes get upset. It's part of the human journey. Accept it and move on.

You're learning.

I'm guiding you.

Your essence is timeless spirit.

Chapter 7 - Losing Worries

In the awareness of my presence, you know that it's silly to worry.

You'll worry less frequently as you get accustomed to living in the awareness of my presence.

Why worry? It accomplishes nothing.

Why worry? Will it change anything?

There's nothing to worry about.

Are you feeling weary and burdened? Rest in the awareness of me.

You can either worry or trust me.

Regardless of appearances, everything's fine.

Everything's Divine.

Don't let your heart be troubled.

Put your trust in me.

Don't worry about your life. Don't even think about it.

Go beyond thoughts.

Throw your worries into the infinite ocean of my love.

Before long -- you'll be gone.

Is something troubling you? Turn it over to me.

Everything happens for your good.

I'm your life.

I'm your strength.

Whatever it is, I'll handle it.

In me, you deal well with everything, because it's me, not you, who is dealing with it.

I'm acting through everyone involved in the situation.

I act through everyone and everything.

You're in my loving care.

You don't have to figure everything out.

You can't figure everything out.

It doesn't matter why.

It is what it is.

In the awareness of my presence, you know that there's nothing to worry about.

Leave everything to me.

Chapter 8 - Losing Regrets

In the awareness of my presence, you know that regrets are as useless as worries.

Regrets serve no purpose.

What was, was.

What was -- brought you to what is.

What is, is.

I make good come from everything, even from what you think might have been your errors or bad choices.

I heal whatever was done in the past.

Whatever happened, happened for a reason that is beyond your ability to understand, but it was meant to happen. Of that you can be sure.

If it wasn't my will, then it wouldn't have happened.

Live in the awareness of my grace.

Everything is meant to be as it is.

Be at peace in IS.

I've ordained everything.

Nothing happens by chance.

Everything that happens is meant to be and it's for your good, so be at peace.

You're one with me. I'm the essence of you and of everyone.

In conscious union with me, you're in my kingdom.

In my kingdom, there is no looking back and there are no regrets.

Chapter 9 - Being Real

In the awareness of my presence, you're real.

You don't conform to the illusions of the world.

You're in reality.

I'm the only reality.

Why pretend to be something you're not?

You are who you are.

There's no need to act the way you think the world expects
you to act.

You don't have to 'fit in.'

It doesn't matter if you fit in or if you don't fit in.

Live out of the timeless, infinite center of your being.

Live out of the truth.

Knowing the truth sets you free.

I'm the way, the truth and the life.

I'm within you.

I'm expressing -- through you.

I'm light.

My light shines through you.

I created you to be you.

Can anyone be a better you than you?

In humility, you're the real you.

You're the you who I made you to be.

I love you unconditionally.

In the awareness of my presence, you're humble. You are who you are. You're real.

Chapter 10 - Being in Reality

In the awareness of my presence, you're in reality.

Love is reality.

I'm love.

I'm reality.

There's no fear in love.

In love, fear vanishes.

When you're in fear, you're in illusion.

Love yourself as I love you -- unconditionally.

Love others as I love them -- unconditionally.

Love me as I love you -- unconditionally.

Love heals.

Love just comes natural in the realm of the supernatural.

Reality is supernatural.

In the awareness of my presence, you live in love.

You're in reality.

Chapter 11 - Delighting in Life and Love

In the awareness of my presence, you delight in life and love.

You delight in me.

I delight in you.

I'm not mad at you.

I'm not disappointed in you.

I love you, just as you are, right now.

My love for you is infinite and eternal.

You don't have to make yourself better in order to be loved by me.

I made you.

I'm expressing -- in you, through you and as you.

I'm in everything, and beyond everything.

I'm life. I'm love.

I'm within you and around you.

Be conscious of my presence, always and everywhere.

Delight in my omnipresence.

See me in everything and everyone.

Observe my will in everything that happens.

Loving me means trusting me.

I'm love, and I love you.

I'm the IS of all that is.

Detect my will in the happenings of each moment, in every detail of your life.

My love is infinite.

Love cannot be limited or contained.

The love within you can flow to anyone anywhere, even to those you've never met or seen.

In love, all is one.

You came from love.

You'll return to love.

You live because of love.

I'm love, and I'm everywhere.

In me, you too, are everywhere.

Be mindful of my presence always, and delight in life and love.

Amen.

Total Gratitude

Total Gratitude

To you, my friend in Spirit.

Contents

Introduction

Written from the point of view of God speaking to you, Total Gratitude is about giving thanks to God for everything -- just the way it is, and for everything that happens -- just the way it happens. If you'd like to use the book for daily reflections, it's divided into thirty chapters, one for each day of the month. Peace be with you, my spiritual friend.

Chapter 1 - A New Creation

Turn your will and your life over to me.

Having turned your will and your life over to me, you've started a new life.

The old is gone.

The new has come.

You're a new creation.

Live with an attitude of total gratitude.

See me in everything.

Chapter 2 - A Silent Sermon

Where did you get the idea that your earthly life was supposed to be painless and easy?

Take up your cross each day and follow me.

Be dead to yourself and alive in me.

Be patient and peaceful.

I'm your refuge and your comfort.

Look at things from a higher view.

Be thankful for everything that happens, because everything that happens is my perfect will for you.

Let the way you live be your sermon.

Chapter 3 - Live By Faith

Live by faith in me.

Be calm in the midst of the storm.

Loneliness leads you to me.

I'm taking care of it.

Leave it to me.

You can't control what happens, but you can choose how you react to what happens.

Choose gratitude.

I make all things work for your good.

Chapter 4 - Be Content

Be content with all that is, just as it is.

Marvel at the mystery of it all.

Delight in sunsets, rivers, forests and streams; in starry night skies and mysterious moonbeams.

Be thankful for everyday blessings.

I know you intimately.

I created you.

I love you -- and I like you.

You're a means through which I'm expressing myself.

Chapter 5 - Live and Let Live

Let others live how they choose to live.

Everyone has their own path to travel and their own lessons to learn.

Let others live and learn.

Live your life.

Explore your path.

I'm taking care of you and of everyone else.

Put your faith in me.

You don't know what's best. I do.

Live your life and let others live theirs.

Chapter 6 - Ongoing Discoveries

The spiritual journey is one of ongoing discoveries.

In the wilderness of silence -- you hear my voice.

In the school of suffering -- you draw close to me.

In the forest of darkness -- you learn about trust.

In the tower of solitude -- you meet celestial friends.

In the house of humility -- you become aware of reality.

On the open sea of total surrender -- you discover true freedom.

Chapter 7 - Wisdom and Love

My wisdom and love are one and the same.

Consider how blessed you are.

Appreciate all that is and all that happens.

You're not better or worse than anyone else.

You're neither more nor less enlightened than anyone else.

There are a lot of ways of looking at things.

Love is the right thing -- every time.

Love everyone.

Treat others the way you'd like to be treated.

Chapter 8 - Come to Me

Come to me with your troubles and burdens.

Come to me with your sorrows and fears.

Come to me, even though you've been lost for years.

Come to me, though your sins are many.

Come to me, though you feel unworthy.

Come to me, my prodigal daughter.

Come to me, my prodigal son.

Come to me, no matter where you've been or what you've done.

Come to me. You're loved and blessed.

Come to me -- and rest.

Chapter 9 - Seeing the Good

Delight in my will.

Give thanks in all circumstances.

Having gratitude in all situations shows that you trust me.

Seeing good in yourself, you see good in others.

Being joyful, you bring joy to others.

Accepting yourself as you are, you accept others as they are.

Being peaceful, you bring peace to others.

Knowing my forgiveness, you forgive yourself and others.

Knowing I'm within you, you know I'm within others too.

Chapter 10 - A Channel of Love

Be a channel of my mercy and love.

You can be helpful and kind while still having an attitude of holy non-attachment.

Leave the results to me.

Give thanks for everything.

Be quick to forgive. I enable you to do that.

Enjoy fellowship with your heavenly friends. Commune with your spiritual friends who are on earth too -- including those you've never met or seen.

You can be wherever you want to be.

Love travels infinitely.

Chapter 11 - Humility

Be content to be a nonentity in the eyes of the world.

Lose yourself in me.

Surrender -- completely.

Quit trying to control things.

Quit trying to control people.

You can't control anything or anyone.

Give thanks for what is, just as it is.

Rejoice always, and leave everything to me.

Trusting in me is the essence of humility.

Chapter 12 - Grace and Truth

Grace and truth come from me.

I'm the way, the truth and the life, and I'm within you.

Live in the reality of love.

You're free -- because of my grace.

See me in everything and everyone.

Be unattached in your doings.

Get out of the way.

Watch things unfold -- within and around you.

I'm in every situation.

Chapter 13 - Where is Your Faith?

Where is your faith?

Totally abandon yourself to my will.

Trust in my divine providence.

Be thankful for all that has happened.

Be thankful for all that is happening.

Let go and let me.

I'm handling everything -- perfectly.

I'm looking after you.

I'm providing everything you need.

Chapter 14 - The Inner Shadow

Trust in me, and see my glory.

I dispel the darkness.

Get to know your inner shadow.

I know all the shadowy areas of your psyche.

What seems dark to you isn't dark to me.

I know you better than you know yourself.

I'm the essence of who you are.

I'm Life and Love -- expressing through you.

Chapter 15 - The Light of Love

My light shines in the darkness -- within you and around you.

Wherever you go, within or without -- there I am!

In the light of love, everything is different and new.

In the light of love, what seemed dark isn't dark anymore.

When light shines on the shadow, the shadow becomes one with the light.

You're the person I made you to be, and I love you unconditionally.

Mystical union with me happens in humility.

Chapter 16 - As You Are

I know everything about you.

I brought you into being.

I know the dark, hidden corners of your psyche.

I know every facet of your personality.

I love you as you are.

Just be your real self -- the you who you are in me.

You're a spiritual being having a human experience.

Chapter 17 - Wonder and Beauty

Consider the wonder and beauty of it all.

The present moment is filled with mystery.

You're in the midst of the miraculous!

See my spirit when you walk on the street -- shining from the eyes of everyone you meet.

Be like a little child -- trusting and spontaneous.

Be totally dependent on me -- and be in my kingdom.

It's going to be a beautiful day.

It's beautiful right now.

It's always a good day.

Chapter 18 - Compassion

Accept yourself with your weaknesses and flaws, and accept others with their weaknesses and flaws.

Be compassionate and merciful toward yourself and others.

Everyone has insecurities.

Give me your loneliness, your sufferings, your inner turmoil and your pain.

I transform you.

Cast your cares on me.

Move the veil of your mortal perceptions aside and see me.

Chapter 19 - Praise

Gratitude is the expression of your trust in me.

Being abandoned to my will, there's nothing to complain about and nothing to criticize, nor is there anything to worry about or anything to regret, because you know, by faith, that whatever happens to you at each moment is what is best for you.

Be full of praise, always and everywhere.

Will what I will.

Receive happily whatever happens to you, knowing it's what's best for you.

Chapter 20 - Be Gentle and Humble

Be gentle and humble.

Forget yourself, take up your cross and find your true life in me.

Keep dying every day till your dead.

Love everything -- just as it is.

Love everyone -- just as they are.

I'm guiding you and teaching you through your human experiences.

Let your only desire be that things happen the way they happen and you'll always be happy.

Chapter 21 - It's All Me

Be perfectly content with what is.

You're already in the realm of infinity and eternity.

You can be anywhere you want to be.

You can be with whoever you want to be.

Watch things unfold -- effortlessly.

Apart from me you can't even exist, much less do anything.

It's all me.

Chapter 22 - Like a Little Child

Apart from me, you're powerless.

Apart from me, you're unable to manage your life.

You can't control anything, so quit trying to be in control.

Entrust every aspect of your life to me.

Be like a little child.

Depend entirely on me.

Welcome to my kingdom.

Chapter 23 - Give Thanks

Be thankful for everything.

If someone gives you a gift, give thanks.

If someone steals from you, give thanks.

If someone welcomes you, give thanks.

If someone shuns you, give thanks.

If you're healthy, give thanks.

If you're ill, give thanks.

Nothing happens outside of my will.

Whatever happens is my will, and whatever I will is for your good, so be thankful for all that happens.

Chapter 24 - Healing

I heal the past -- whether it was twenty minutes ago or twenty years ago.

I'm making the path ahead straight and smooth.

The awareness of my presence heals and brings peace.

Humbly admit your sins and move on.

Forgive yourself and others as I forgive.

Be at peace, no matter what happens.

Whatever happens is what is best.

Keep your mind on me.

Do everything with humility.

Chapter 25 - Everything Is a Blessing

Your life is a wonderful mystery.

Everything is a blessing.

I'm in control, in every detail of your life.

Do what you do, while trusting in me.

I'm within you and around you -- whether you feel my presence or not.

Live in a state of perpetual gratitude.

Chapter 26 - Right Here, Right Now

Right here, right now -- this is it.

Your essence is timeless spirit.

Be at peace, knowing that whatever happens, moment by moment, is what is best for you.

Give thanks for your present situation -- just as it is, in every detail.

If I didn't want you to be where you are, you wouldn't be where you are.

You're exactly where I want you to be.

Chapter 27 - All is Well

If it wasn't my will, it wouldn't be happening.

If it's happening, it's my will and it's for your good.

Whatever was, is and will be -- is perfect.

Everything's the way it's meant to be.

Give thanks for all that is and for all that happens and be at peace.

It is what it is.

It's all good.

No matter what is occurring, all is well -- always.

Chapter 28 - Thankful for All

If someone treats you unfairly, give thanks.

If someone is generous with you, give thanks.

If you're rich, give thanks.

If you're poor, give thanks.

If someone is rude to you, give thanks.

If someone is kind to you, give thanks.

Be thankful for all that is -- just the way it is.

Be thankful for all that happens -- just the way it happens.

Give thanks for everything.

Chapter 29 - Everything's Sacred

The things of this world, whether perceived as good or bad, don't matter.

You're not of this world.

The awareness of my presence is the healing influence in every situation.

Your awareness of me touches other souls and sparks the same awareness in them.

In me, you see everything differently.

Everything's sacred.

Chapter 30 - Living in Gratitude

Living in total gratitude, you're blessed, and you're a blessing to others.

Whatever happens is my will, and whatever I will is what is best for you.

In me, you have peace.

My peace I've given you.

I'm love.

I'm in control.

I'm the only thing that's true.

If you'd like to say a beautiful and powerful prayer, simply say -- Thank you.

Amen.

Thank you for reading Divine Reminders.

This book is available from Amazon.com and other retailers.
It is also available on Kindle and other devices.

If you have a question or a comment, my email address is:
sjcurran100@hotmail.com

Many blessings.